A Kiss Upon a Universe

Romancing the Unknown

John-Robert Coleman

Written & Published by John-Robert Coleman
Edited by Lolane Girard
Cover and Book Design by Liane Rich
www.LovingLightBooks.com

First Edition
A Kiss Upon a Universe: Romancing the Unknown
Copyright © 2016

Heart Card Productions LLC. Honolulu, HI. 96830
www.heartcardproductions.com

ISBN 13: 978-0-9718638-4-2
ISBN 10: 0-9718638-4-9

Available at:
Amazon - www.amazon.com
Barnes & Noble - www.barnesandnoble.com
Also on Request at Local Bookstores

This is an infinite kiss upon you the universe; not
knowing to where,

to when or to whose cheek this may land, maybe
it'll make you blush.

John-Robert Coleman

You may use a bucket, shovel or spoon

for I do not discriminate how much you should

dip from my inexhaustible treasure chest.

The gifts I offer are eternal,

within you and for you. Just ask.

The Universe

Foreword

This is a compilation of paper trails of love notes and inspirational thoughts. They are results gleaned from several years of texting daily ideas each morning to circle of friends.

The ideas herein are both metaphysical and down to earth. They are colorful gems mined and radiate from the one same Universe. They can for an instant disperse rays of light like facets of a diamond. They arrive as observation, home spun prose, free verse, proverb, wisdom, lyric, dialog, vignette, story, commentary, bit-humor and other author quotes, to name a bundle.

Eloquently stated by Jonas Salk, *"It is always with excitement that I wake each morning wondering what my intuition will toss up to me, like gifts from the sea. I work with it. It's my partner. "*

I am grateful to the Spirit of Kid-Heart-in-me whose work he loves is word play.

These writings can serve as insightful, guilt-free reminders into our true nature, our innocence. It brings great joy and gratitude that I become its courier to offer these gifts to you. May these readings open your heart and mind, to lighten your burden and to brighten the trail on your journey...

"One must share what is natural to one's heart…"

In search for right answers

there truly is none.

One already fits perfect in this dream, and

"You have not lost your innocence.

It is this you yearn.

This is your heart's desire. "

Quote From A Course In Miracles

Find no stranger, only lovers

home in the dance,

for laughter has no fear

o' paradise found

undrape my soul

with sweet simplicity;

imagine you as

gift to someone grateful

be blessed by one's love.

From Pearl Drops of Aloha

Universal broom

sweeps clean the mind's debris,

as leaves bow down to you

and flowers open slowly in the sun

for you;

growing-up takes patience

and one need not push the river,

be as water and

your path will be made plain

find one's oasis...

Fountain of ideas

bubble up,

flash flood of insights

as living words

from divine wellspring

stream rapid to brain

and pours forth

to one parched thirsty soul;

I desire to immerse myself

in an Infinite sea

dripping towel

soaked with joy.

A Rendezvous With a Nameless Lover

I have a lover who resides within me and I have just met her, though she never introduced herself.

So I asked of what was her name? She said, *"I could be whoever I wanted her to be"*, and added, *"What are in names but merely different labels for ONE source."*

Then I asked her, *"When did you ever move in because I thought I was the only one paying the rent here?"* *"I've always dwelled within you waiting to be discovered."*

I asked her wondering how after all this time she is so patient. She solemnly replied, *"I always enjoy loving you for who you are no matter what, and that is why I AM That I AM..."*

Why then did it take me so long to feel your presence, to discover you? She knowingly said, *"I was always at the center of your being."*

Now tell me how come... or what makes you so, so sweet? To my surprise she repeated one word three times, *"Practice, practice, practice."*

I told her I desired to hold her in my arms and I pleaded with her to never leave me again and she explained something I will never forget, but often do, she said, *"It would be you who would forget me and I truly never left you."*

I began to thank her for bringing this indescribable joy and heartfelt moments we were experiencing together but she said nothing and just beamed...

In gratitude I offered her a red rose as a token of my love and asked her to what I believe the most important question ever to ask of another being, I propose, *"Will you ... will you marry me?"*

Poised with divine smile, *"Oh you silly being... I already have."*

Sprouted in beauty

flowers spring petals

blossoms are we

Aloha leis stringed together

as eternal buds

where rainbow hues flourish

and the hula Ti-leaf palms

dance to gentleman's desire

to read

between the folds;

our instruments breathe

vibrant light and sound,

music is her name.

From Pearl Drops of Aloha

Ask oneself,

how many steps it takes

to get where i am?

How much time it takes to

arrive at this moment?

How much effort is required to be

what I am that I am already, and

who is this pretending not to know

what one already always has known?

One of saddest

mind-set of our underworld,

"*not good enough.*"

and who told you were less than

beautiful, whole and complete,

and why compare?

Heaven knows only One-of-Kind,

now please go kiss the mirror.

Watering roots

nourish all aspects of trees

and to rise

they go deep, and

while winds gently caress

and whispers of freedom to be,

love breathes love.

Swells of anxiety

may raise guilt from past or fear of future.

Hey, those are idol characters in our play,

illusionary dead beats

hanging out in corners of our mind,

lost essence of presence,

kiss them good-bye...

Will anyone really care

to count

those moments

it rains on our pillow?

In our mind's eye

building a life is

under

construction

and

de-construction

at work

making endless corrections.

"Once in a while it really

hits people that they do not

have to experience the world

in the way they have been told to."

Alan Knightley

Fluffy our thoughts fleeting

like transient clouds

they play around the sun for a while

and make for unreal puffy stuff

at times dark clouds, nightmarish thoughts

are pranks to a happy dream--

we make up the thoughts as images

that often disguise reality or

reveal the truth.

The truth is

never separate

and what one seeks

one already is;

and often forgotten

we continue to play hide and seek,

wage war and peace on ourselves

although our split-minds can amend.

Man's hope is to forgive,

Peace reigns silent.

Self-shining

ever-fresh,

presence awareness

is our true nature.

In our inherit *knowingness*

somewhere in depths of our psyche

we intrinsically know

everything is One in the same.

Finding that ideal work

skin tight over one's spirit

you are well-endowed;

you can't help but pour

your soul into it!

Have I not told you

or you may have already noticed by now.

It is not what one achieves, what one acquires

nor what one does for a living;

save just *BEING* who you truly are.

When one is touched by unbounded love

it will embrace wholly

the grace that is the Spirit-in-you

knowing forever the backdrop

everything is the same

for within this gracious gift we all bestow

expect nothing, appreciate everything.

Rumi aptly points out,

"Beyond all appearances

there is a common essence of our true nature,

Listen, out beyond ideas of

right and wrong, (our dual world)

there is a field, I'll meet you there,"

and someone will arise

appearing as a dream character in our Play,

and He will post reminiscent reminder,

a sign on gateless gates --

this is iT!

as dreaming a dream continues *you are iT!*

With much love to you from yourself,

Celebrate your reunion...

I discovered

this being is not monogamous

but attached to non-attachment

clinging to be free;

oh I can be a cling-on

then I am not,

maybe

a knot on the loose

or just foot loose.

Upon our stepping stones

on hallow ground

we are afoot

by tiny step by step

day in and day out

we do be do

bit by bit,

we be

of service,

blessed abundant.

"...I am not present;

what Presence is, I am.

I am not aware;

what Awareness is, I am.

I am not love;

what Love is, I am.

there is no 'other'

that can be liked or disliked.

There can be no 'other'

to either thank or implore.

So I cannot say 'I love'

but rather 'I am in Love,'

inside Love..."

From "Perfect Brilliant Stillness" david carse

Yes I have a love life

because that's all there is...

Sitting home alone?

Hey, come and dance

and hear His song;

shake off that fear

wiggle your butt

then maybe you'll

bump into someone

to warm your cold feet;

and maybe

humble your heart.

Our upsets are ego's set-up,

just laugh, let it have its fling

and like all of us who pass wind,

wafts never last, and

So now let's go on this Ego Fast,

let's quit feeding what is really not there!

Say swissssh!

Imagine

the sky, a veil

earth, a footpath,

at center,

One-Heart-beat.

Fear knocked on the door,

love answered.

Turned out to be no-show!

Love knocked

and love itself open the door,

love is the answer...

Why settle?

Let's keep your vision, aspirations alive!

Spread those sheltered wings

and create with the Creator.

Miracles begin happening and

continue to do *pono*, the right thing.

Live your own endless love notes and poetry

if not for the sake to re-call our innocence.

You know who you are...

The Universe

I dreamt

being a mere dot on a map

in unfamiliar territory

traveling on bumpy roads

that led everywhere and nowhere;

navigating through maze of contradiction,

swimming in ocean of appearances,

meeting with unknown dream figures,

exchanging one dream state for another,

playing hide and seek, sow and reap

and here I am--I start and finish here.

Where else could I be?

Where else is there for

this spot on a map?

I am vital part and

particle of a Universe.

Should we meet

you may very well awaken

in me that which lies dormant, and vice versa.

This merely is recognition we are not separate;

we teach each other what we need to learn

from each other,

we awake from the dream.

So what is this mysterious ever-present iT?

My guess is rather than effort, strive and strain

to be 'some-body'

we may well be content

to consider humbly being 'no-body'

for there will be no one home

but the ever-present iT,

that's peace brother.

You're iT !

One is not created

as a perpetual medical experiment.

Consider oneself

radiantly healthy,

whole and complete work

of indivisible

artistry,

wholly

good

and beauty-full.

Let's say

no death exists, and

nothing forever can be threatened,

and who so ever has

no worry and

never been born,

never have died,

Is already enrolled

in Eternal U;

however, some students

will insist on academic grades

for approval or acceptance,

and if one must,

you are already

anointed, blessed A +.

"What could you not accept, if you knew

everything that happens,

all events, past, present and to come,

are gently planned by

One Whose only purpose is your good. "

Quote From A Course In Miracles

One is either

ego-driven or spirit-driven;

though you can only choose

to get behind the wheel of one,

but not the other.

Either help drive out suffering

in the world in some practical way

or forget about everybody and

let go of the steering wheel;

turn inward to the true Source of all compassion.

Decide one or the other.

To find freedom or not

simply ask of oneself?

"Am I at peace right now?"

Angels I believe abound in disguise and

do not advertise their wares or whereabouts.

They seem to play quiet roles, no claim to fame

and appear with impeccable timing.

I surmise they serve in a divine light-hearted way.

I am certain you have met one or two

on the road on your journey

that be worthy to acknowledge.

Dare to unmask yourself,

I know you will come clean...

Consider this pure of heart:

The art of loving

and for it to stay

it has to be given away.

To live this day all is a miracle

the angels do further say,

"Come fly with me and

I'll be by your side from dawn to dusk "

and around and around in joy we'll glide

as we chat about this and about that,

play show and tell, sow and reap

unfold each moment we'll share our earthly stories

and may we be filled with grace and wonder

for in my joining with you

here on this page or in our passing

submersed within these idol words

is '*love and true forgiveness*'

and to regain our wings is to continue to amend;

choose again a fresh start, and

oh… it's not easy to be pure of heart.

The mind can be a beautiful instrument

for one who plays it through the heart with heart,

because one can feel it. Soulfully.

True teachers are in business

of disillusionment of

undoing what was truly

never separate in the

First place, that's purity or innocence.

Since we are housed in this bodily-shell

we may be accused

of living in the House of Paradox

and Contradiction

and we'd all have to admit,

yes and no.

Oh I get it, then I may not?

It appears no one likes

to mentally lapse,

be unaware,

forgetful

feel lost

alone

even though one does know

it's only a short-lived experience.

One may perceive or consider

in any of its varied forms

as guilt-free space

where innocence lives.

Should one not understand

this itty-bitty-ditty,

it will happen naturally

and this too shall pass.

Within A Tear

Trapped within a teardrop

was prideful bits of fear;

because of all the love growing inside

it had no other place to hide.

No longer could it contain itself

so something had to give, and

any given moment

tears will fall from our bodily shell;

where upon a kind voice

out of the blue will remind us,

"Have you not noticed after a rain,

does it not bring bursts of sunshine?"

Suddenly a rainbow peeks through

our misty landscape

as if a sign there is hope not lost, and

within each teardrop there be a thousand

rivers that flow to heal not you alone,

but for an Holy instant

drown many of our illusions

into an infinite sea of innocence,

we but weep for return to our real home.

When finding oneself in muddy waters,

I am told to let it be, let it settle onto its own.

But for God's sake, please forgive yourself.

Who wants to be a *'stuck-in-da'-mud?'*

Swipe that mud off these shoes;

go mud-less, and

just maybe we'll run barefoot together.

To this being

the word

'en-light-en'

means

' to make light of '

as fire flies

take

themselves

freely

into the

evening

dusk

beaming

to their own

delight,

bringers of light.

Each leaf

that makes its

gentle fall, and

may it release

each worry we have made

fall gently

into peace...

In a metaphoric way

oyster yawns this morn

from deep sleep to awaken us

and from that tiny, shiny pearl

is symbolic of the you and me;

and should we spot another oyster

along the way and it drops a pearl,

open our hand and heart.

The quickest entry

to one's heart is to tell the truth,

that's love's doorway to everything intimate.

Now please go open those doors and windows,

Breakdown those walls and fences,

defend nothing

grasp nothing

let Love

breathe you In...

When this being no longer *thinks* he is

the centerpiece or someone special,

look to the impersonal Great Sun

that constantly shines.

It's presence radiates through

everyone and everything.

Created from the One same Source

one need do nothing

but listen,

be you radiant,

innocent

and please stay here

and let's get a tan.

There really is no sunset;

we merely pull down

our eye lids

to rest awhile...

One can accept and honor people

right where they stand,

otherwise

we'd be the self-accused,

stealing from our very own innocence.

We can complain less, bless more.

Allow love to tread with us in gratitude.

Anyone can easily be an arm chair visionary.

Eventually one must rise from one's seat,

either to walk the talk, to take action

to not mind what's happening right here.

Why place ourselves in prison behind bars?

To be happy we can cut through our judgments;

and here is the *KEY* to a clean breakout,

the only escape plan--

forgiveness is our hacksaw bar none.

A Letter

Be it my own expectation, my observation
be it real or imagined,
I can't help but to feel, to write you
and this too I pray and candidly say,
stirring in your heart I believe a passion
can be awakened.
Still I observe there resides within you
a lonesome love,
an untouched love that asks of itself
to be joined here.
This precious gift, a talent that you have
may be buried, denied or forgotten
and how dear that you are to me my friend.
One must share what is natural to one's heart
and so my precious one, come forth and play;
A magnificent love song is seeking you.
It is as near as your free will to choose
to renew a love that will always find a way.
Not to fear, the path is still open and clear
to those who will thirst to hear you play.
The Universe

61

Our journey together

no one can really rain on our parade;

for out beyond our right or wrong footpath

on this earthly plain

we all march to the self-same Drummer,

and at times we may stumble and fall

still we can sing and the beat goes on...

Off the Wall

...Dark splatters upon the wall

and shall we wipe them clean till we

erase them all;

they are fear based spots... ... ...

of unforgiven thoughts, and

while we are here

It is not for us to condemn

yet to find within and clear

the blemishes to love that

reveal the light

of our innocence...

we can gently do the inner work

by clearing of one's mind--

swipe away those past hurts

off the wall

till condemnation be no more...

Catch the drift,

anything we send out

is meant to boomerang,

return to sender.

You are not a puzzle looking for its pieces.

You are wholly love, the one you been looking for.

If one knows of man's dualistic law,

one is either lawful or unlawful citizen.

With Universal Law one is

Imbued with Spirit

ideally in a non-dual world

there really is nothing to obey.

Be an in-law-of-Spirit,

no outlaws dwell.

A strong spirit

transcends rules.

Happiness is not a pursuit.

It is our mind's shift-work;

to make internal adjustments in attitude,

to an acceptance of '*all that is*.'

"The idea there is a *problem* ...

that's the wild hair in the ass of humanity."

Adyashanti

View these passages

as waves

that meander by and

be a passerby

as we experience together

our ebb and flow

we ultimately

will come to the calm

rest on an open field,

the eternal now...

Funny or ironic--

all along one is gifted

with a passport To freedom,

but we doubt freedom From what?

and somehow we'll discover no one has

or ever will issue an expiration date

on how to soar, to be free.

Inside wonderment, inside joy or inside love

there's truly nothing to figure out.

Our One-Mind-field

is never made for

'boots on foreign ground,'

but to bring peace

to our own home,

that's inside you.

Sometime we need clarity:

to '*raise the roof*' to get out of the cellar,

that is, to shed light on our misperceptions

of dark idols, idiotic and bully thoughts.

We can simply change our mind about them,

leave them in the cellar

or bless them and say goodbye!

The secret to enlightenment

is that there is none.

We just forget

to raise our lantern,

to turn on the love-light.

Dig this!

One cannot earn or buy

a ticket to heaven

for that would be in vain.

Are we not seen as

unconditionally

'good boys and girls?'

Hey, we just want to go and play

in His beautiful garden.

Oh I can dig that!

Love of Your Life

Roses are red; your eyes may be
blue, green or brown
as this poetry I bring will never end.
Within this dance
whirls an infinite romance
and let's face it eye to eye—let's be real,
sometimes one can be crazy or twisted as a screw.
While in my daily walk I do think of you
and please know what is truly offered here.
Should you feel worthy of one's own heart's desire
and to further should our passions care to merge,
call it what you will--the best is yet for us to see.
Meanwhile let's thank our Creator for this crazy
endorphin-hormonal-glue,
and because of this strong urge to meld with you
I am at risk of being bold and a crazy fool,
but so what?
You may think this too warm, fuzzy goo -
No, this is about someone
who we often overlook, and
I invite you to go to the mirror.
Meet the '*Love of Your Life.*'

Since *'life is but a dream'*

It appears one may have series of flings;

though in retrospect we'll come to

realize love is always the lesson.

Let's draw from the depths

of our sustenance and strength.

Let's sip from our cups of gratitude together;

empty our neediness from our desires.

Let's un-cap this evening and

get drunk on the living waters

with some fruitful conversation

and laugh

till there's nothing left in our cups

but love running wild...

The puppet Trickster asked Tricksy,

"Why is it that we are always on a string"?

Tricksy replied, *"Cause God planned it that way;*

He cannot live without us

and we cannot live without Him"

"Oh, said Trickster, *ok…let's get back to work"*

Here is One string

that always loves to draw you near

for you to have a ball,

to play with joy--

Love is, and nothing else is.

Spirit is, and nothing else is.

Go no further, have a ball!

Here's an idea…

'I do not know anything.'

Nothing sticks to me

and should this get real sticky

I can always ask of myself

to become unglued,

the solvent is self-forgiveness.

Even the greatest story ever told

seems to be of eons past,

gone away

yet it still remains imprinted.

We are forever the Holy Grail

walking each other home.

In my company

there is nothing I want from you

but to be yourself.

So join me at the

center

of a laugh

in beloved joy,

call me Friend...

Flashes of brilliance overcome this being

on occasions as a reminder:

It's not of me, but through me

that I am grateful to be able to send His light.

By no accident I am very glad you

showed up here

for this momentous reception...

Your path may appear

different than mine,

although for the both of us

in the short-run

it's merely about our 'preferences'

and in the long-run

will not make a speck of dust difference

when viewed on our Home-screen

of eternity...

Awake

With regard to those *lies* I bought along the way,

let's flip them upside down to right side up--

the truth is in the *undoing*, not accumulation.

Please let's stop all payments of spending on

petty illusions and worldly toys.

May I peel back the masks

from my imagined idols,

arrest this egocentric clatter and

chatter, this noise,

this busyness we think is all that matters.

Let's invest in seizing the calm.

Embrace our love-light;

step out and raise our lantern

so others may wake

in the power and glory of

the Spirit-in-you!

From The Messages of Peace

Sometimes I cannot stomach my own words

the pangs of intellectual indigestion;

while an overlooked, shelved prescription

calls for a daily dose of Vitamin B-Quiet.

The ego is like a crack in an egg shell

that can never be born of itself.

Love can only know nothing but itself.

We can view this world as friendly or hostile.

We can opt Not to make it real,

that's why clowns were created.

A Halloween World?

Everything is dream stuff where dream character's show off and parade in various layers of masks, appearances.

Be this my own movie I project on a screen of 'nothingness', yet we have been taught to sing of hope '*merrily, merrily life here is but a dream.*' and why we would care to see Halloween scene any differently?

It is easy to dismiss masked faces as disguised non-sense; yet it does appear to be a whimsical circus acts filled with fun.

Besides acting out of dream character in a dream is not far from the truth; we do daily exchange mostly unconsciously one mask/role for another anyway.

Be that said, one can enjoy Halloween every day either as a merrily magic treat or see it as hollow trick; whichever, it's still all dream stuff in our Play.

Stepping out of character into another for a change can be an out-of-ego, thrillingly therapeutic experience casted as temporary release into another inescapable dream creation; a wonderful excuse to enjoy life now.

Yes, let's bring in the clowns, laughter is healing.

Pauses between each heart beat

is somewhat similar

between every inhale and exhale;

be it miraculous,

custom-built-in

they are peaceful rest stops on our journey

and should we retreat to our favorite hide-out

as we sometimes will

we yearn for inner peace.

Most self-help programs are based on

some form of inadequacy or unworthiness

until one day one will come to a cross road,

to stop, to listen,

to perhaps experience this *ah ha* moment,

"By God I am the affirmation! "

Oh it's easy to be an imperfect being.

The penultimate truth is we are perfect beings

living in an imperfect world.

Yes the world has it upside down, it says,

I am a sinner and I need to improve, instead,

I am a perfect being but I need to *unlearn or undo*

some illusionary ideas

about myself that I *think* are true

but are self-made false images, and

whoever transcends these limits

in anyway merely becomes more natural.

Any effect one experiences

is really a cause

to what one draws to oneself,

Intention + Effort = Results

Love doesn't hurt unless

you give consent to it.

To take leave sometimes

can be an act of love,

to replenish one's soul

and return or move on...

The only thing we can offer each other

is inspiration...to awaken that sublime

essence within ourselves.

I can only offer you

the light from my lantern to yours

and from yours to mine;

Bring light to light, fire to fire,

Be a beacon in someone's storm.

To give all to all

every veil must fall

into the mystic

while His heart does dwell in you

given all to all

and

when you invite me into your heart

I will be there.

Otherwise,

I will wait until you have change of heart.

The Universe

Stand on His Rock

Truth is true,

solid be you too...

Rock on... rock on...rock on...

no waivers issued,

no options offered

Stand on His Rock

Truth is true,

solid be you too...

Rock on... rock on...rock on...

Welcome to:

"Conversations That Do Not Matter"

(Formerly the Nothing Seminar)

Sponsored by Nothing-To-It-Productions.

Guest Lecturer: Professor Not-a-ham.

Location: No-Where-ville.

Time: Now, at your own leisure.

Seating: Unlimited, right here where you sit.

Cost: Priceless or out of sight

This Premiere event you have just experienced

Promises to be non-imaginative, no brainer

and may go down in history

as nothing we care to recall.

It appears I am a repeater

with you in our classroom

and if you'll notice any absentees;

some students may have just graduated and

they completed all lessons needed to be fulfilled.

Others may have ditched their assignment

or none of this really ever occurred;

and to whomever reads this-

you have class.

Words lost their meaning

before they are expelled;

yet the sound of silence

whispers only of your holy name.

Can one seize the Creator's job?

For countless eons

thousands upon thousands

of people have tried in vain, and they still do

until one becomes aware that our all-loving Boss

was the First to issue our first 'Time & Space Card,'

'I am as my Employer created me'.

When the Creator winks at you

it is a good sign

He is flirting with you to return home.

Be on the lookout...

Wink-a-dink-ado!

To fuel our faith, ask for a fill up…

and keep on pumping a happy trail.

Your Eternal Gas Station Attendant

There is no such special favor as

'Chosen People or *Culture.'*

"God chooses those who choose Him"

Quote by Paramahansa Yogananda

To err is human.

To our inherent innocence

nothing happen.

Everyone has an opinion,

and this is one of them.

"Laughter is the glorious sound

of the soul waking up! "

Hafiz

Whatever baggage one is carrying

it will be with you

until one chooses to find a dumpster.

Drop it off here for peace sake!

Signage on Dump Yard Fence

For a win-win.

File for 'No-Thought' Insurance.

Silence is the settlement. Peace the outcome.

With gusto in our youth

we did set off many of orgasmic bombs,

but now as elders we are just pleased

to be fire cracker's in bed.

Confession from the Ole' Gang

To tap into the Universal flow

it is you that must turn on the faucet.

The most succinct, practical advice

I ever received was simply,

"Stay with God."

Open your heart

Yet do not accept tokens.

To befriend with our Creator

is to be truly practical.

When something resonates as Truth,

it is meant to be extended, not contained

and that's why one such phrase, '*Pay it Forward*'

came to be... there you go...

Words are worldly symbols that keep on

chasing me around and around the block

until they find an altar at home.

And all the while indelibly written

at the center of my being,

a four-letter word.

To our birthright

Spirit knows of no thought

as love knows nothing but itself,

for that's who we truly are--

original, natural, spirit.

The world isn't all sweetness and

bouquet of roses, though consider

'lilies of the field' where there is no

struggle or argument,

only peace on the green.

One's destiny can change overnight,

that is,

I am just happy to wake

to anew day!

"Don't ask what the world needs.

Ask what makes you come alive and go do it,

because what the world needs now

is people who come alive"

Dr. Thurmond Howard

Love lifts me!

We rise by lifting others,

the yeast of life...

Most worldly news broadcasts

are man's shadow of recycled conflict/separation.

The Good News is that one can mindfully choose

not to make it non-fiction.

Wherever we may be we can choose to

line our pockets with happy seeds,

inspirational ideas to sow, to disperse

and to cultivate

in the rich soil of our mind's garden.

We'll reap a prosperous harvests and

be as farmers,

they do it naturally.

From Johnny Heart-Seed

Trees remind me

I am

of the same leaf

of the same branch

of the same root

sowed in the same

fertile soil of

love made manifest of itself.

Let not religious views be better than

or less than any other.

The Spirit-in-us is of unbounded innocence,

because the All-Seeing is only

infused with love and light

and knows of nothing else, and

like you, love shines magnificence.

Would it really make

a thread of difference

if all of us were spun from the same fabric?

Meanwhile, as the soul fits

we can clothe it with love and service.

Here is the secret:

There's none...

A ship upon a sea surface

may have lost its bearings;

unlike a wave in living waters

can never abandon its Ocean.

"I wish I could show you,

when you are lonely or in darkness,

the Astonishing Light

of your own Being!"

Hafiz

In a non-dualistic world

all there is what is happening to no one.

When it's discovered there's no one,

there's just celebration of aliveness by no one.

There is only *Being,* and this will be repeated

throughout--love is, and nothing else is.

The earth is reverent,

and within its measure of treatment

resides how well we first treat ourselves

and our inhabitants, our humanity.

There is no escape hatch

one can hide under.

In Truth

there is no trying,

nor shades of gray

or excuses--

one does it

or doesn't,

either it is

or isn't!

When we get ourselves

out of our own way,

"...everything is beautiful

in its own way..."

What's the rush?

Yield to a happy day,

allow someone the

right of way.

Inside prosperity

you are a precious,

priceless being through

the eyes of the Sacred.

I have a full cup

that always desires to pour into you.

Do not forget this...

The Universe

Limitless can be

another word

for eternity, and

why worry?

There are really no Stop Signs

or Dead End streets

on our sojourn,

unless you put up a road block.

It is beautiful when you find someone

that is in love with your mind;

Someone who desires to undress your conscience

and make love to your thoughts;

Someone who desires to watch you slowly take

down all the walls you've built up around your

mind and allow Her inside your beautiful heart.

Author Unknown

Place no labels

on anyone or anything;

or you'll be held prisoner

in corner of your own cell block..

If it doesn't resonate in

the heart, it's not.

When it does, one will experience

chilling moment

fleeting experience,

and shed tears of gratitude

from something greater

than the me-self.

In *Reality* no one is

never left behind.

The door is never closed

and forever left open

and She'll always keep

the porch light

on for you...

While the Sun

always keeps on beaming,

our thoughts create

the images

we choose

to view

either

sunny

or

cloudy.

As winds of change make clouds,

so to our thoughts go to and fro,

come and go

still,

all is well and

to *think* all is not well;

well, that too is all is well.

Listen, hear me out--

It is this I will always say to you:

Please know this goes beyond all

the wonderful doing's that I witness

you already do and will ever do for anyone,

I can only love your being

for just being, being you...

The Universe

No mind, no matter.

No matter, no mind.

I may have lost my mind

and I have no intention of

retrieving it.

No mind, no matter.

No matter, no mind.

Simple math:

Addition is an accumulation.

Subtraction may be the solution.

Create a space,

eventually it will fill up again.

Minimalist Mind.

Ultimate Truth is:

*nothing to prepare

*nothing to become

*nothing to overcome

*nothing you don't have already

*nothing that can be added,

*nothing that is missing;

however, when someone offers

you a gift *I Do Not* recommend

you say, "*Thanks for nothing*!"

No matter how huge or tiny

one can always unwrap that gift

you have been carrying for too long

and simply give it away,

your divine light...

You are the creation. This is freedom.

"I am created to create the good,

beautiful and holy."

Quote From A Course In Miracles

Here's the real buzz!

Nature continues humming

its happy, eternal tune whether

we hear it or not.

The Creator loves circles and

we all are in circulation, in service--

busy-body-buzzing-buzzers!

Take a pause in nature;

observe how birds perch upon a limb.

Witness how quickly

they move on...

Whatever you think or say to one's mind

the Universal Mind will always respond

with a resounding *YES!*

It's our friend or foe

and that's affirmative!

When one discovers the ego is not the doer,

you'll have knocked on Heaven's door

and have forever found a divine friend

whom you can always count on.

What's amiable about authentic

friendship is

we have nobody to impress.

Just BYOB, Bring Your Own Butt!

Heaven knows you've always been invited.

We do not know of the challenges

that weigh upon another's heart,

and to be of kind-heart--

now that's our opportunity.

I am flat out making all this up

like these words on this page.

It is from an acquired mind

that house my collective experiences,

beliefs and habits and I project them

on the screen as my own image

and label them as my identity, self.

Also I am told we are really first an eternal spirit

living in a human form awhile, and

even so, while on this earth plane it is still wise

to look both ways before crossing the street.

I am entitled to miracles as I am *mis-stakes*

although the latter is mistaken for the former.

Simply said, there are no mishaps and

just know everything is in Divine Order.

When the world is pulling

me in all sorts of directions,

there is now and always will be

this convenient tool

I can use to quail the mind's imaginary onslaughts:

Transcend and be still and there will be an answer.

"To the mind that is still

the whole universe surrenders."

Lao Tzu

My real story?

Ideally the short of seemingly long version is

this process of getting out of my head and into

Her heart is my true purpose;

that's till it empties itself into nothingness

from which it came for there be nothing to prove.

Right now, I am here with you

romancing the unknown.

Feel empty, send love.

I may not always be a ray of light unto Thee;

however, I am grateful the Sun does always radiate

constant.

His love is for everyone and everything.

To speak of Ultimate Reality there is *'no other'*

in this Universe.

Oneness cannot be understood

by this body-mind, so I let go of the unfathomable.

To my surprise at this writing

my biological Dad came to me in spirit

and I always had boyhood

memories of our good times together

fishing and the many fish we caught

my Dad voiced this as I scribed,

"I am pleased of my son and I have since realized

he is and always will be my catch of the day,

and I notice too he has grown to be a good man. "

Signed, *ELC and Your Beloved Father*

Be not a doormat to illusions, idols and tricksters

for they do not have a permanent address.

Only love welcomes us home.

Hey, some people will understand you

while others may not and

that's perfect.

What remains constant is the Spirit-in-you

that never has left you,

and no worry

you are not alone.

Beside you with each step

is a thought of a prayer to be found,

He walks with you and me on Hallow ground.

In case you wondered:

Universe = You

You = Universe

And a kiss, is a kiss is a kiss.

I open

my heart today

to find you here

all the while

at

its center

beaming

like a star

that you are

and to this

by you

given of

your light

away

to the

One,

I choose

to stay aboard.

We can truly hold only One key to the Universe

and to those that remain on our key chain;

they open, unchain or unlock doors

to the service of our Divine Estate.

A babbling brook will ultimately stream

to the depths of a quiet pond.

It's not of one's status, degree or

station in life that matters;

it may well be what emanates from the

midpoint of one's being that adds indivisible

healing presence.

In A Wink (Lyrics)

When you awake from your sleep, prepare your
wings to meet the sky...
"*Oh young eagle, today it's your turn to learn how
to fly,* the Elder did say, *"I can see your heart's
willing; see the green light in your eye, oh young
wing one, today you are ready to join the morning
sky* "

There upon the mesa cliff edge they both stood
and the Elder did say, "*I'll give you a sign when to
take to the sky,*" and within a wink of an eye
young eagle takes to the morning sky and oh how
she's making heavenly spins and gliding on high
winds and heaven sang out,

Oh fly young eagle, oh fly oh fly...
there is freedom, freedom on high
Oh you can fly, you can fly! fly young eagle, oh
fly... fly

Now young eagle's Elder did finally say, *"I see blue sky reflected in your eye."* and in farewell sigh young eagle departs in wink of an eye, spread its wings showing off her heavenly spins and soaring on high winds and heaven sang out,

Oh Fly young eagle, oh fly, oh fly
there is freedom, freedom on high
you've made your home the sky
Oh Fly, oh fly... fly away...

In true flight

as the soul soars

so goes the heart

and to where this may land

I have no idea

but I will surrender

to Spirit more abler

than the 'I'

I met myself at a

local Oceanside Café

and I journaled this in my notebook:

"I got intoxicated on life today,

Tropical Pure Mana and

I believe Aloha was the local

reverent name brand...

I abstained from ordering diet water,

Instead, I took a dip into the Ocean.

It's a wonderful life!"

Nothing is simpler than ONE,

not in a numerical sense,

rather we are One

of His descendants.

Pride

is ego's subtle

disguise in dressing-up

to feel momentary bloated.

This passage does nothing,

Can you?

From one's crown to one's heart,

feet and hands,

may we play it as we feel it;

because we are the instruments

of light and sound in the dance.

Our lives are truly between

ourselves and our Creator only.

The remaining stuff is temporary

busyness of drama, pomp and puff.

May we like it but not be of it, and

while we are having fun

with our spins upon this stage,

let not our busyness detract us from

our real bottom-line business at hand--

to love and to be loved.

No one can turn their back on you or anyone,

unless one *'thought'* less of oneself.

"I am affected only by my thoughts."

Quote From A Course In Miracles

This is simple,

when we thirst

we go to the

His well

for

it calls out

to us

and for us

each day

we drink,

we live.

We are lost in the melody

that sings to us of

hearts that have been broken

and only love and

forgiveness can mend, and.

when it appears something

or someone snuffed out our light,

it may well be we need

just refuel our lantern…

The answer is not found

in seeking Mr. Right or Ms. Right.

Our courtship lies always within the bed

of one's own heart and

sharing this is merely choice;

and I know some of you know

this as pillow talk,

others may see it as meditation and prayer.

aahh...for heaven's sake,

let's open our hearts anyway!

Give up browsing!

Everything that has

or ever will be written

is already

rooted in one's heart,

Go there.

A Lullaby

From my heart to your soul, here we are.

Oh I can see, oh I can see it in your eyes

you are a star of one sky,

ray of light of one sun

reflection of one Mind,

always the light shines through, already good

inside of you

for you'll always be a reflection of mine, and

will you remember, remember who you truly are?

In a mirror of God's perfect light, here we are.

Oh I can see, oh I can see it in your eyes

you are a star of one sky,

ray of light of one sun

reflection of one Mind,

always the light shines through, already good

inside of you

Oh I can see, I can see it in your eyes,

forever you'll be a reflection of mine, and

will you remember, remember who you truly are?

This is not about 'you or me',

for peace lies in those

quiet, empty

spaces

between our words.

Listen,

for there

is no

peace

like Home…

Imagine

to view

through these

innocent eyes;

having to

experience

a sublime

encounter

with our

true

origin,

the First

and Last

instant,

forever

bliss...

We are infinite

spectacles of light,

part and parcel as mortal

shifting grains of sand

we celebrate on boundless shorelines

for being lived in a dream

we are moved to serve;

for we are really One in the same,

colorful aspects of nature

and I am thankful

I am neither alone

nor at the center of this

diverse Universe.

At the clearing of our mind

is an open field onto forgiveness,

as each blade of grass has

at its root,

the beauty of its own,

seed of innocence.

See the awesome beauty all around us

And that *'unknown'* is the constant

and everything is a sign, ' *To Be Continued.'*

If one does not understand this,

let it be an eternal mystery

while it goes without our thinking

does fuel, breathe and move us

by the grace of Spirit,

thrive on unconditional love... *TBC*

In this Home School without walls

one cannot be graded.

Freedom is truly knowing

we belong, we are welcomed and

we are honored in the *'I am presence.'*

And

our presence is like

a splash in an eternal ocean

of a Divine idea

that ripples to boundless shores

of the unknown.

It's never too late for us.

We always have

something to give of ourselves.

With our acts of kindness

We are in circulation--

here still longing to serve,

to contribute.

If one should *'wear one's*

heart on one's sleeve',

it may be considered misplaced.

Please place it back where it belongs,

at its center.

From Lost and Found

Gravity may pull us down.

May this idea have you stand up straight.

A Parent

To this melody

that keeps playing

in my head;

and to the soul

that already

knows of its

dawning

may it awake in me

to sing this refrain

from my center

to your heart,

and in the reverie

of our soulful

moments together

and upon that sunrise,

the daybreak

of this poet's release

you listen

and she smiled that smile,

we let it be Our Song.

To You: The Amazing Little Seed That Can

In one's garden is sown an eternal seed

you choose to be love, and

with daily silent care from within

you envisioned a way to make it grow

and flourishes as a heavenly bloom

a Holy radiant being namely,

(Recite your full name here)

A light onto the world,

A miracle to behold

and I am glad you are here.

Like you I am also seed sown

in an open playing field

harvest inside love

as beloved friend,

for I've always known you to be

that amazing little seed that can....

The Universe

We are the light

through our Spirit's eye

for our Creator has neither

blinked nor rolled His eyes,

forsaken our holy presence...

"Has it ever occurred to you

we are seeking God with His eyes."

Quote by Adyashanti

oh breathe something

into this soul...

may I be an open vessel

fill it with your Presence,

Essence, and

let it be ever so clear

for I always know you

are always near

for we breathe

the same air, and

may our journey

be with care

never to be apart

because I now realize

you never left my heart.

oh breathe something

into this soul...

I do not know of my destiny

and it appears I am going somewhere,

moving through space and time;

although I am certain

I am birthed

for a Holy purpose, and

by the sound of our Spirit's delight

She is always

calling to us,

talking to us

walking with us

guiding us home...

And God said, *"Love your enemy"*

and I obeyed Him and loved myself.

Kahalil Gibrand

Where it is not found in one's head

it can be discovered

at center

of one's own heart.

This is the residence of our infinite intelligence

and you certainly came to the right address.

Love is an active noun

can trigger

an active verb,

Love Is.

Simple, we are sentenced only

to noun and predicate.

One can choose to doubt

and live a half-life with

a split-mind,

or choose to live

with full faith

in One Universe

that doesn't mind at all.

Living on a cushion

or *'pins and needles'*

one cannot experience

one without the other,

but you can certainly

feel the difference.

Why run and hide

from love we have to give

that never left us;

and surely

how can anyone take from us

what our heart now desires

be given away...

So let's

pour our love-light into night

empty our love-bucket by day,

best we circulate this...

One can be no less or no more

'than a bright star,

as pure as light,

as innocent as love itself.'

We have it all to radiate.

You are that love-light

And know

anything less are just shadows

in need still

of your holy light,

that's why you are still here.

The Universe

Now is

forever timeless,

one without second.

Everything

unfolding perfectly

as we are moving figures in a dream

yet nobody can truly share

in words

sowed in silence of now,

ever-present awareness.

With all that we think

must be done

or undone

through the grace of Spirit

I want to spill my cup

until it empties itself of all

I can forgive

and so be it

life delicious

to the

very

last

innocent

drop.

To that race to the roof-top

in search of that something special may be futile,

as vain pursuits to nowhere.

To remove those illusionary rungs

from our alleged ladder to success

is to step down to earth

and rest upon the lawn of forgiveness.

Realize there is only One goal

we gladly give up the chase

for inner peace...

"There is no one in human existence who

is not your soulmate, and

there is not one person you encounter

in your life you will not see again,

think about that."

Excerpt from Emanual's Book

When our search is truly over

there will be truly only ONE of us,

and nowhere found a form or mind

will discover there is nothing to iT!

Our intellect

does not have anything over the Divine.

The heart knows the soul better

than the mind,

and "I am fascinated by your words

but where we truly join

is in the silence behind them "

Quote by Ram Dass

Legacy is not something we leave behind.

Consider *'what does love do now?'*

Oh at times life will *appear*

or feel like it bit us in the ass.

Again, dare we ask kick,

'What does love do now?'

From My Sore Rump

We are stars

wrapped in skin

looking for

the light

of our innocence

that has always been within.

This poet, artist in me may not find the deep you,

Yet I continue to choose to reach within

to His bottomless Well Spring

where all is universally abundant.

May joy rain upon your shoulders

and the sun always place smiles

upon your face and leave not a wrinkle

of regret that we have met

at the center of a laugh or two

for only our souls do know

our way is one of grateful heart.

You are the gift

to oneself,

to someone,

to others.

The universe exists

because of you.

Remember that

and be glad.

The Universe

I spilled some love today

onto your table,

And the heart said

to just leave it be,

let itself runneth over...

Those who leave everything

in *God's* hand

will eventually see

God's hand in everything.

What if after you die, God asks,

'So how was heaven?'

Epilogue

Literally, there's truly nothing here to grasp,

save you pass it by with a kiss...

A Kiss Upon a Universe:

Romancing the Unknown

John-Robert Coleman

Available at:
Amazon – www.amazon.com
Barnes & Noble – www.barnesandnoble.com
Also on request at Local Bookstores

Also by John-Robert Coleman

Pearl Drops of Aloha: Oh Hawai'i My Hawai'i
Song of Forgiveness; Ho`oponopono (YouTube)
Affirmations for Awakening the Creative Spirit (CD)
The *Original* Heart Card Deck

Heart Card Productions LLC.
PO Box 8319, Honolulu, HI. 96830
www.heartcardproductions.com